Hypergraphia and Other
Failed Attempts at Paradise

New Issues Poetry & Prose

Editor   Nancy Eimers

Managing Editor   Kimberly Kolbe

Assistant Editor   Sara Lupita Olivares & Alyssa Jewell

New Issues Poetry & Prose
The College of Arts and Sciences
Western Michigan University
Kalamazoo, MI 49008

First Edition, 2021.

ISBN-13 978-1-936970-71-1 (paperbound)

Library of Congress Cataloging-in-Publication Data:
Metsker, Jennifer
Hypergraphia and Other Failed Attempts at Paradise/Jennifer Metsker
Library of Congress Control Number: 2020940738

Art Director   Nick Kuder
Designer   Emma Wiest
Production Manager   Paul Sizer
          The Design Center, Frostic School of Art
          College of Fine Arts
          Western Michigan University
Printing: Books International

Hypergraphia and Other Failed Attempts at Paradise

Jennifer Metsker

New Issues Press

WESTERN MICHIGAN UNIVERSITY

For my parents.

And for those who are struggling with mental illness. You are not alone.

Table of Contents

Acknowledgements

alice blue review: "Sand and Flowers"

Banango Street: excerpts from "Days of the God-Sized Brains"

Birdfeast: excerpts from "Release"

The Dialogist: "To the Actor Who Plays Me in an Educational Video"

Gulf Coast: "Dark Helicopter"

Hobart: "Not a Walk on the Beach"

The Journal: "Delusions of Reference in a Dark Room"

Nightblock: "Deus Ex Machina" [Light bright envelope] and "Deus Ex
   Machina" [Soaking up]

Okay Donkey: "Dialectical Argument with Boyfriend and Birdkiller"

Poetry Daily: excerpts from "Release" (from Birdfeast)

Really System: "Beta Waves Are Not Part of the Ocean and We Prefer the
   Ocean"

Rhino: excerpts from "Release"

The Seattle Review: "The Furies Leave Los Angeles"

Two Cities Review: excerpts from "Days of the God-Sized Brains"

Whiskey Island: "Why I Still Use My Dead Pet's Name as My Password," "This
   Is What It's like to Lose Time and Ask for It Back in a Letter"

wildness: excerpts from "Days of the God-Sized Brains"

I wish to thank Scott Beal, Jocelyn Gottlib, Alana DeRiggi, Ellen Stone, Anne
Carson, Megan Levad, Robyn Anspach, Courtney Mandryk, Brendan Ritch,
and Kendall Babl for their support in the creation of this manuscript.

Hypergraphia and Other Failed Attempts at Paradise

It's the dereliction of stray facts,
the furry heat of them,
that makes me chase half-truths.
I'll write anything fanatical
to make me forget this tortured life
of canapés and calculators and corsets.
Those starfish, those creek swallowers,
those dangerous words
and collisions with the past.
The suffering of nonsense seems like fun
until my room is being terrorized
by birthday cards, prosaic stars, the fleecing
of our pensions, the phony fruit,
the hungry tongues, a wetted stone
for sharpening our fingers.
I cannot see handshakes for what they are,
turned clay, handmade,
because hands are everywhere,
washing off the viruses.
Fill a super collider with balsa planes.
Witness all the planes colliding.
Then there is Canada with its vast ice plains.
Then there is water and no water.
Moons come in a variety of colors.
But there aren't enough pillows for everyone.
There aren't enough soft landings. There aren't enough
drink carts or cave dwellings.
There aren't enough trees or heads
on Easter island. There aren't enough mysteries
to make this interesting.

Dark Helicopter

When the dark helicopter descends over the neighborhood
we must duck down and cover up the flower beds

as the water from the bird bath catapults its skeletons.
The lawn breeds black spikes in the oppressive geometric

shadow of the helicopter. This is how they grew the nails
for the crucifixion. When we say *this* it has an extra layer in it.

Dark helicopter believes it is an improv coach. It shouts
its auto-message through crackling speakers: *Say yes!*

It's the same crackle of unwrapping the mints we keep
in our jackets to remind us there are no dark helicopters.

There are balloons, planets, puppies, snowflakes, mini-muffins,
but not this wood paneling and this water cooler and this yellow

legal pad and this man holding up his hands to describe
a new addition to the library. But hands up happens

and the helicopter becomes the hands and hands
become the helicopter. This is what the mints are for.

I'm in a conference room under a broken umbrella,
which is to say I have reservoir on my head

to catch the dark weather falling from the helicopter.
Stupid insomniac helicopter threatening to turn

my blazer into salsa. *You can do this!* shouts the helicopter.
In a four-way mirror full of conference rooms,

a million rooms goose-stepping across my backyard,
a man leans out of a helicopter with a megaphone,

and the swings whip around, and the roses bleed,
and I offer them a tissue. Dark helicopter

tries to convince us it has a rainbow inside of it,
the same way an oil well hides rainbows

inside of its elbow grease. *Work harder*, yells the helicopter,
You can do it! You can be a productive member of society!

while it blows the trees sideways and slices up
the neighborhood into all the spare parts

that humans are made of.

Why I Still Use My Dead Pet's Name as My Password

Three feet beneath this soil
there lies a dead pet.

I breathe the pollen that blows from the flower stem
that grows from the head of the dead pet.

The perennials are more intelligent now
with their roots in the dead pet's
brains.
                    The flowers watch me,
                    their roots in eyes.

Bury me here
in the blue gray of this rain today, in this field
of buzzing blue bottles,   on this blue-flamed
afternoon.

The voices tell me
I should be ashamed,

but my fingers pet my dead pet's name
into the blank white spaces
where complex codes cascade
                    into their corduroys

and arrange themselves inside of rooms
                    too small for furniture
                    or photographs,
                    rooms too small for pets.

I know the people in

these rooms. I met them
in the ether.

They turn on televisions, their fingers
fidgeting with the blue light,

blue as twilight, blue
                     as mermaid fins
                     and finite.

In the blue of oncoming
advertisements,
they're calling up the faces of their dead pets
in marigolds and wagons.

                     The little Ingalls girl
                     goes running down the hill
                     in her bright blue bonnet and the world
                     expands a bit.

A man in a blue suit pushes
blue pills through a window, saying sleep now
and be silent.

                     There's only one android
                     in this blue world,
                     and his pale skin

emits a blue light
like a spaceship. Sleep now,

in this fortress, beyond the blue-skinned body
guards, where coffins leech their secrets into the air,
and the air leeches its secrets into the cars, and
the cars pull into garages and breathe.

                                           Sleep now,

in this blue regard,
where pets curl around blue feet,

and where I've gotten good
at word puzzles.

Say something
backwards.

Say something
missing a handful
of vowels.

Beta Waves Are Not Part of the Ocean and We Prefer the Ocean

1.

You tell us there is so much love,
the sun exploding on the sea,
the viridescent little stalks
squeezing through the earth,
the smell of rot and plenty,
but this room has three blue walls
and an opening for spies.
We do not go gently into a night
without prime time,
                                circle k,
                    coffee stains.

It's ontological,
this rumor that the television must be on,
that it will stop
violent voice boxes at dawn.

2.

All bets are off when the wailing begins.
We are bloated by the orderlies in
their algae bloomers when
the gods come whirling in,

                              scrubbing
bubbles,

              comet.

We must divide and carry
cleaning products to shout the grass stains
out of sad tigers who lost the ball game
to an after school sugar-coated
snack. There's no escape
from being a tidy cat.

3.

There's nothing special about
extra leg room in a desert.
The nurses commandeer the remote
because these cathodes must not
disturb our pharmaceutical

bunches,   clusters,

                    charms.

I have stayed in hotels that were kinder
though no sleep inside their basket-weave
coverlets, ice buckets cupped over ears,
yet louder squabbles here, dynamic rinse cycle
as we clasp our hands for egg-shaped
particles dancing sideways
and the cross-hatched grass beneath
a sale on a wheelbarrow,

          feed your lawn,   feed it.

It's April out there
in the yards of all our neighbors.
They must be dead by now,
every lawn we own.

4.

Today only, one day only, epic
tale, tidal pull. Pixels churn
and paw litter, fresh curls mustachio
over cgi mouths,

                  feed your lions.

We are cat lovers
as we float,
the breakers like heavy blue

                       mall cops.

Which heart breaks down doors?

Can it be a cavern of fear
or a mental cartwheel
or an idling engine?

They say that lions don't purr
because they roar.

5.

There's an ocean at the end of the corridor
where the eyes have little squares in their apertures
and the squares have four pink eyelids.

White noise would be a blessing in disguise—
we could sing about waves
that are not   nature,

oceanspray.

Electric string chorus swells into
smell lines and   unhappy meals.
We have not forgotten   the drive thru
is open.

There's a little window here
but no way out

for this   hatchback
of sad tigers growing sadder.

This Is What It's like to Lose Time and Ask for It Back in a Letter

Redaction falling moon;   redaction
isolation room;   redaction
thunderclap;
redaction   crisis intervention
tablets;   redaction
                                     how I
wrote to you
of dixie cups and birch trees
and nurses shuffling   their
paperwork
redaction;
                    tongue drought
redaction;
flash flood   redaction;   the murmur
of redaction;   the cannons of
redaction;
I was   the bible study   wunderkind
in the corner of   redaction;
                    I paced a lot
redaction;
on the lawn   of redaction;   and in
the hall
of redaction;   and by the pool   with
its unplumbed depths of redaction;
                              and the flowers
of redaction,
those thick black stalks   I picked;
so fragrant;   a lysol bloom of
redaction.

II

Release

My father photoshops the word "waterfall" over the waterfall in the photo. In case I didn't know, in case I had forgotten. I admire the word waterfall, a clothed thing. It clambers over rocks, turning natural tricks. If only I could forget about the megachurch over the hill with air-conditioned legs inside. If only I were thirsty or had a vestigial pail. It's like whale watching, waiting for my return. Or like waiting for the rain to put out fires in a megadrought. Palm fronds rattle their accordion hands as I open up my megamouth to accept my share of ashes.

The ballgame crackles from a tiny television set and shoves the sky into a pocket. My father stares at the air as if there were a ball there. There's a gelatinous substance on the steeple, there's a gelatinous substance, I'm sure of it, though I've never been up there. Now I'll never know love again and love will never know me because the world is a scheme and a scheme cannot lift a saggy liver-spotted hand from a hymnal.

The little light in the microwave oven comes on when I open the door and it's such a relief not to think about how little things work, like the frozen things invented by men with degrees in taste who study the desires of the tongue and approximate, approximate. How I heat them! Behind every curtain, behind every cupboard, a chasm yawns open to expose the underworld. We shouted verses in the common room until the doctor said, "Shut up or the moon will turn purple and the world will end." Is there an anecdote here that is worth its weight in salt? I throw a pinch over my shoulder for good luck getting out.

We met in the common room with the psychiatrist who asked us riddles. "What goes around the world and stays in the corner?" The answer: a postage stamp. The secret answer: us. We had traveled far together, burrowing in burial mounds and backstabbing bibles. The pay phone in the hallway would ring in the night and if I picked it up, I would be the prank caller no matter what. Words were candy-boxes. Words had creamy centers. A little sweetness turned the heat up and the parking lot shimmered. On the day of my release, my father gave chocolate-covered strawberries to the cheerless staff who had strapped me to the bed.

At night I want to be told stories about bunnies. Bunnies that go to school, wear clothes, fly planes, play instruments. Bunnies that hop to school each morning carrying clarinets in hard black cases. The bunnies try to play a song together, but they produce only squeals. They ask their music teacher, why is this so hard? There comes a pause as long as the fence that keeps the rabbits on one side of Australia. Certainly talking was hard at first too, the music teacher said, but you didn't stop talking.

If I ever manage a mental health clinic I will try to ensure that the waiting room signs don't have any double meanings: *Have a seat! Your therapist will be out to get you soon!* A fake philodendron gathers dust in a mauve vase, the mauve of the eighties, and a wall clock has ticked itself askew. White noise blows by unused, a seaside conversation driven by the difference between prolific and productive. A productive wind builds mountain after mountain. A prolific wind jangles wind chimes hanging from the eaves.

My father drinks bourbon in the backyard while I circle. Ice cubes clink as they relax in the glass, but I cannot relax because nothing stays solid forever. A man at the hospital in a striped shirt and plaid pants could see UFOs "all the time" and "right now, in fact." A woman said, "Girl, don't believe anyone wearing stripes and plaid." I'm waiting for the day when I've forgotten the fabric and the texture of all that, when there's nothing left to see but an old rotting barn that hasn't been used for hundreds of years. But I have no use for barns. The red barn in my head is not a real barn. I once saw a gray barn, the sooty rain-colored wood maybe was red once. No, I cannot lay claim to any barns.

My father leaves me sections of the newspaper. I scour the obituaries, but they have no specific plans for me. So I stayed up all night to write my will and testament. I gave away a lot of little things like a teacup and a toothbrush and a handkerchief. What does a life look like? A glorious life? A tongue. Otherwise, life can be so vast and boring. If I could have given away subatomic particles, I would have. The kind with the parallel universes inside.

The bunnies study the surface of the moon and try to determine whose face it is. Their first and only guess is God's face. The moon is big enough for two of us, but how could I believe that God would ever dream of giving me so much room? Now the rose buds are blooming on the fence out back, but it's like calculus, trying to make an adage out of nothing. The sugar in the sugar bowl hardens into a rock to represent one idea of patience. It's like the blackbird that fills a parabola with pebbles to get the water out again.

My father does crossword puzzles in his armchair so he can fall asleep inside a word. He doesn't worry that he won't wake up even after all the nights he watched me charge around the yard like a rabid thesaurus. I said anything in my head and in my head was *Holy! Holy! Holy!* and *Arkansas* and *Blake-light tragedy*. Did I tell you Ginsburg visited me? He stood beside me at the dinner table and said, First thought, best thought. But he was talking about death, not poetry. Was I dead? No, because the plates kept coming.

It's a round robin, the endless conversations with my father about commercials. Did you see the one with the donut head? Or the cat who opens doors? Or the woman on strings like a marionette? Then the basketball scenario, the back and forth across the court. It was March. It was madness. All of this happens on the couch. Wrap me up in a slanket or a snuggy or a bumble bee suit. I plan to sit here until my eyes only look open.

Do you know what it's like to sit at a desk with all of this in your head? There's a keyboard carved out of wood beneath my fingers. It takes a chainsaw to write a single word. I try to sit very still as if there were a contest. Out the window, many fine young bird finding worms. The file cabinet is such a sad companion with its files full of trilobites pressed into the rocks. When the phone rings, it sounds like a lamb bleating. I hate staring at myself in mirrors, especially in the public restroom, especially on Monday, especially right after I have small-talked my way through another lie about my weekend.

My father brings me sandwiches, but what I need are syndicated sitcoms. Glassine across the table, eyes skating across a blue lake, sick blue, and the room lit by laughter echo yellow glare and God is in there somewhere. How I wished every word out of my mouth could be a word that I'd seen before. How I wished every word out of my mouth could be a water balloon.

Bunnies dressed like mothers wash their children in basins. Dwindling daylight. They stand upright on hind legs and scrub. A dark cloud passes over the basins and the little bunnies begin to cry. The mothers say, don't worry, one day you'll forget all this. What is there to remember anyway? A bunch of days like dried flowers? The chasm that swallowed up the flowers? The telephone polls that lined the chasm shouting *I I I,* asserting their will against the sky?

As I trace the sickness back, it's children who I see playing house. I was the father and the daughter. I was the daughter and the stranger. I was the stranger and the angel. I was urges, nothing more. I had a journal full of notes on this, but my father buried it in the yard beneath the lawn ornaments, the spinning flowers, the woodman sawing wood. Fragments of conspiracy fly up from the garden bed and land on the surface of the pool. My father gets the skimmer out and scoops up the detritus to a smooth jazz accompaniment. At least I know my name again. My name and my planet.

My father, who is not in heaven, smokes on the patio. My father, who is not in heaven, says, it's over now. Skirt and scar, scar and skirt. I have a little cart for hauling wood. I have a chopping block. And the God swallow, the hard lump? The past is a looking glass lodged there, a gilt frame resting on the larynx. Past participles.   Pangaea. Praire grass. And all those scary bits, the voices before dawn, the loss of dawn. I can't admit that all these things have an underlying hum.

III

Sand and Flowers

To see a World in a Grain of Sand / And a heaven in a Wild Flower, /
Hold Infinity in the palm of your hand / And Eternity in an hour
—William Blake

1.

Flowers bloom. In my brain, flowers.
Flowers bloom. The mind is a flower,
a season, a rhythm, like a stalk
of a flower bends and breaks and fills, lifting the weight
of a furious blossom, the heavy head of a mind flabbergasted
by the beauty problem. It lasts
through the night while angels sleep on their silent halos,
streetlamps on a damp night. An uptick
in numbers presents itself as a promise, then removes itself
in a failure to anticipate the sum. Flowers fall down on graves,
consolation prizes for the dying who I dream of fondly,
their long walk down a familiar corridor, their shuffling gait,
their gowns brushing floor tiles.
The corridor is littered with red lips, petals
I longed for once, a honeymoon of petals, a palace entrance.
I counted my steps in a death dance while the waters of the world
dried up and the dog kept his distance. I could have been dead.
There would have been flowers.

Walk with me along the shore
where some see misery, some see a catastrophe of sand.
Golden beaches swirl up and spin into hourglasses.
Some see misery, some see
whatever God wants them to see
as faces turn away again, faces turn away.
Clock gears tick off seconds in a chest
until the glimpse protracts into the folds.
The day parodies the glimpse,
then resolves itself in satire:
cake batter, battery charger.
None of the pleasantries or not so pleasantries
exchanged a glimmer with the same color gold.
Then nothing is gold.
The grayness of the sidewalk. The pseudo-black highways.
The correlating shapes shift their weight
and try to speak.
They are mostly restricted.

3.

Flowers made of sand blow into the back room
where waiters loiter on a break
from an eternal shift. Flowers made of sand
at the tables where philosophers sit saying *if if if.*
I once held a marble I thought was the world but it rolled
between a crack in the floortiles. I once
wrote a letter to God on a petal, but minutes were hours
and hours were flowers. The trees outside whisper
their tragedy: they knew Jesus as a child.
The floor is a long dark metaphor, sandblasted. No one
brings me flowers. Electrical towers
stand watch over electrical boxes and eternity
scooped into a lunch tray, eternity billowing in a curtain.
Why has God hidden his message
in grit and impossible medallions?

4.

St. John walked on the shores of Patmos,
the white sand beaches
mimicking a body wrapped in a shroud.
A number of shapes require
dire pronouncements, like the numbers
themselves, the references to Revelations, the sand
and the flowers, those paroxysms of joy and woe.
The grain of sand produces nostalgia
for quantum abrasions, oh, those tiny calculations,
but it's hard to stick a landing in sand.
Don't wish for eternity here or anywhere dimensional.
Horses gallop in the clouds with roses in their mouths.
A flower can be a heaven and the sand
can be a hell and between them,
a factory of days as delicate as sea foam
and as liminal as dying.
I close my eyes and wait
for the flower petals to arrive.

Deus Ex Machina

Soaking up the burning igloo
of my night light sweats,

I sing a song less disruptive
than the pledge of allegiance.

It's a polyester vibe,
a rodeo joy ride.

Tomorrow will be another story,
another pause by the window

that could turn into a lifetime
wearing cinched jackets.

I lurk on the ledges, watching for
watershed moments,

rectory birds' nests
and fire gods be damned.

When the disco ball comes on
in the cabin,

the sky descends
in hearty platitudes.

But it's different,
how you think of me,

check the obituary,
cheek to shrubbery.

The billboard described it
perfectly:

a suicide hotline by
a slot machine spinning:

jackpot!
everybody wins!

Gericault Paints a Portrait of a Woman Suffering from Obsessive Envy

1.

She covets Gericault's
colored pigments ground
into powdered gems, sly grin:

the same muscles are missing
in animals, they said.

Can he see it in the tuck of her chin
and her lack of wings and her red-rimmed
lids and her bony cheeks and her spider-veins

and the way her eyes follow him
when he packs up his supplies
and leaves?

This little night makes a grinding noise.
Every time a flower dies, God is divided.

2.

The after-effect of flesh is where the soul resides,
but she's nothing like the finch, they said.
To a medical doctor, she might look
like a sow, but a sow doesn't know the grass
is greener in another field nor can it sew
a seam of urges in a frown line.

Is it her missing lip or her sinking eyebrow
or her hooked nose or the rivers furrowed
in her forehead or her bonnet, torn and flapping
like the failure of a white flag
to properly unfurl?

The after effect of flesh is where the soul resides,
but every time a flower dies, the grinding is divided.

3.

Is it his charcoal-colored heavens or
the cannibals who washed up on the shore
or the severed human limbs instead of ham hocks?

The after-effect of flesh is where the soul resides.
On this, they insist.

Or is it
the smell of piss in a cramped and umber corner
from which her soul emerges, a heavy sack
to match her lack of retinas?

It's easy to believe that the night
doesn't love her, but does she love
the night? Does she long for it, or does she covet
hands like haunches
grinding down her skin's translucence,
so fragile, like flower petals strewn
down the corridors?

The doctors wave their heavy
hams around while pacing to and fro,
and the petals in the shadows make a grinding noise,
then die.

4.

Jealous flower,
thin as a petal in a storm.
To be impoverished

and wish is to be
inefficient; if you want
to know want

you can find it
in the heaven
she conjures

where even
God desires
fur like animals

and the after-effect
ripples through
her cell walls

with a viscous
pearl-like
facade.

5.

This little night, this little
grinding expression,
this little woman,
this man with his colored palette,

every time a flower dies, it stains the earth,
and the earth feels a little jealous knowing

just a hint of what it isn't.
Is it the solitude or the doctors
who watch over her or the days
sunken like a terrible boat or the years
that whittle fingers like wood
or the little nights swallowing

the dripping walls in dreams that are uncertain
about the grinding noise or where the soul
resides since it has
no significant features or none she's
ever seen because

she has no mirror,
she has no longing
for a mirror. She doesn't wish
to see her face
when Gericault leaves.

Deus Ex Machina

Light bright envelope, an alphabet of light.
Ancient men in my head, how they called to me
with protractors and carapace equations.

Then came the genuflection,
                              quicksand,
falling into God's hands.

I fell in love like falling apples.
I made phone calls walking circles in a tidal wave
of broken phonics.

I wanted to know how much He loved me
in whale bones,
the time it takes the universe to make them.

Now the world is flat again.
It's a paving stone
It's a ten million piece puzzle.

I put a piece in my mouth.
It tastes like math itself.
It tastes like a broom closet.

The Furies Leave Los Angeles

Dangerous to be big and famous—there strikes the thunderbolt of Zeus!
—Agamemnon

[enter: three old women in a red convertible]

The freeway off ramp
has caught fire.

They must keep driving
into the dangerous sunset,

a dead man in the trunk,
palm trees passing,

light striped like
bars in a cell.

The look on a child's face
when she sees a corpse,

that split second terrain between
brain and tongue.

They cannot halt it.

Someone somewhere
is killing something.

Or letting someone die,
or cutting someone up.

They would not settle
on the worst dressed
as vengeance.

They are
deadly moles. Irritating rashes.

But the rage that drove the action,
it already happened.

It was lily-white,

at least that's what the travel agent said.

[enter: an aging actress]

You would have killed for
the role of the spurned lover.

You would have killed
for the infomercial.

Better than a fade out,
a curtain call
as prurient as a cafeteria.

The ocean view
cannot save you
as it laps at its unlovable
distance,

the moonroof cannot save you,
and the script editors will not capitalize
your lines, which means

the anger is interiorized.

Bless the mother
who raised you because she will
drop off your Goodwill boxes.

There's nothing worth saving
with a face like that.

You're no Cher, no Gwyneth.

You're no endangered fish.

[setting: bedroom, dying light]

You encounter them
in bed,

in the sick sack
of your comforter,

bearing the fruits
of basket weaving,

a grass skirt
for every citizen,

such light protection
from the storm
blowing in.

You don't know

what you did.

A quick scan
of your action items,
reveals your villainous cackle
was
decidedly cunning.

And in the video diary, you made it clear
that you are here to make enemies.

And yet,
you cannot hide from them,

not even in the therapeutic boxes,
not even in a drug-induced coma.

Their quick pulses
clot the

freeways, reptilian
in their heat.

The expeditious are damned
to scaly overpasses

inching up and over
like lover's tongues.

Too many sick
citizens

sit behind the wheel
of misfortune

(i.e. the boiling point).

Blonde-hair tied up,

you have
Bible-thin papercuts.

You're not going to the chapel,
you're not going
to get married.

The options are
shave your head, buy a gun,
play dead.

[setting: the southern hemisphere]

They're flying now,
swooping down below

the tropics
of Capricorn,

Tierra del Fuego,

then off the map.

Canisters of gas
in hand,
they board ships,

they get tangled
in the nets.

Long nights
suit dark imperatives,

Antarctic winds
carry death threats.

How can they avenge the likes
of sleek silver robots

and antibiotic wash?

They can
melt us.

Pink shadows,
pillboxes,

we're
frozen flesh.

[chorus: the furies sing about fate]

Like a fruit basket
not in a hotel room,

like a primadonna
after she stops singing,

we are focused
on the lack,

the perilous hole
in the ozone,

the unsigned yearbook
in the satchel.

It's why feature films
recycle the same actors

while others
serve drinks,

edge lawns,
sell
hemorrhoid cream.

Periodicals
fail, the clip

about the dead baby
reigns on

the weather channel.

[exeunt]

Night is long
like a braid
knotted, barking
dog, hum.

Moon is coveted
by mythic animals
in the underbrush.

Formulas aren't
rich enough
in the mother
tongue.

You fear
old women, you fear

the apocalypse

in your apartment
window.

Would it help if you
put bars on it?

Deus Ex Machina

1.

We pulled into the midnight parking lot express lane
lost in the detail
of the laughing man's face.

We tractor pull umbrellaed
into a nasty night of talking about
the way that cows moo.

If no one harmed us, we wouldn't have virtue.
If no one harmed us twice, we wouldn't have philosophy.
If no one harmed us three times, we wouldn't have
prisons and places like these to save us from

this cookie cutter calibrated
forced entry telephone game
and the cables below ground
serving up their slim offerings.

2.

Don't take this
personally,
but I want you to stop
telling me what to do.

You and your
tent revivals and
terrifying omniscience.

I will rent the tent
and you can do
whatever you want.

        I will bring the wafer,
          and you can share it
                or not.

I will repeat the vows
and you can falter
or not,

        but you know
          it's disingenuous,

the way you never
know my feelings,

        the way you never
          wear my shoes.

IV

Days of the God-Sized Brains

Those days still hover, a parcel of air where the radiator still clangs and red light still pours and the man bends down to check the wiring and sucks in the banging ghost sound just before the building burns down. And the hospital rooftop, that graveled container of tubes like the brains I almost blew. The man with the shaky hands slices the wiring in the stove and coughs out a billow. I need to return to that bundle of air above that burnt corner to retrieve some lost items, but God can't remember what he gave me.

The furthest thing from sanity follows a trajectory like a comet: throw it out, it comes back frozen. I admire the handiwork of ferris wheels, those pink lights fighting daylight. Falling off the planet doesn't sound so bad. Beneath the pink canopy, this room circles galaxies with names I have forgotten. Could I have ditched that place for sunny spaces far away, generous sunlight on stucco walls, parrot cry, trying not to die by mistake?

I added an entry to my diary: why must it always be conspiracy rushing toward the ramrod straight back secretarial pool? The best option is some kind of Disneyland for wayward children. But it was always Devil's night where I was from. See the parade of personalities going by with their licks and kisses for everyone? Rock formations in a fountain, belated valentines, buried bones. Someone forgot to give me a mission.

Paradise thickens in the atmosphere of thieves. I'm stealing shirtsleeves in shackles, turning water into Wittgenstein, when an absence comes calling like an Amway salesman. I offer thanks to the schoolyard girls who could talk about the past all night until the squashed-animal, that way the flesh becomes gray. Repeated phrases in my head love to play with troubled things. Decaf is fine, I said, decaf is fine, decapitation is totally fine.

Propositions baffle me in the night kitchen so I brace myself coming down; since the dawn of time we have cherished hard landings. I lay down the rebar, pour the concrete pillow, rest my head. Underneath the bed, a dusty animal sleeps on a knitted mitten. But the delivery system is all screwed up. I have cannibalistic tendencies and all those bells and whistles, like futuristic time bombs ticking backward beneath my skin.

You want to know what it's like? Lightning bugs that cannot fly sleeping in a coal mine. They are diamonds in the rough, ready to be cut. Forest fires, blackened trees, but what ignites cannot be fathomed by fixing home appliances. Ahead in the darkness, otherwise known as my twenties, the light at the end of the tunnel comes on with a clap! Now I'm standing at the threshold, one step in, one step out, one step in again. What does it mean to be arrested, to identify yourself in a line up? A cornucopia of calendar pages, square roots, each and every one.

Reliable as a courier pigeon, I did my job: i.e. I bought things. I lurched into the theater dressed in my fatigues to cry before the Jesuses. I listened to far off disco planets, crooned to the carpet, carried my satchel. But my religious conversion was the God-given equivalent of wax paper. Nothing ever stuck. Now I'm running from the government down tilt and tumble alleys looking for a place to stow my snow globe collection.

Can you call it practical when a rampant amnesia is the basic principle underlying all the record keeping at the gym? I'm not so much mad as grim. If you can call my bluff, I blame it on the upbeat set, their unassuming nature luring them to water cooler men. They love me, they love me not. It's written on a box top. When the taxi pulls up, yellow bonnet in the rain, I swerve into the swear jar and drop a quarter there. But I never learned methods of delayed gratification. It's like I've been framed for something, murder or religious thinking.

I'm overly fixated on the sin of elevators. They take me back to those early years stamped into the wet cement with chalk drawn love letters and hopscotch games to hell. See how I totter on an exponential line more like an animal than a fairytale or a mountain with a tunnel going through it? Fret pillows. That's what sadness is. I can't get anywhere by scraping on that chalkboard with eggshells. I still call my mother every day. She's such a beautiful shade of green. She's gone back in time to watch my baby steps again.

Appetite suppressants cannot help the lack of wish fulfillment happening deep in the warehouse district. Now the undertaker has arrived carrying his case of knives, carving up a cross-stitch pattern he copied from the underside of leaves. Where did my self esteem go? Into the green things? Into the slippery green? I prefer the ladies, those fast girls in limousines, straddling their daddies. Show me a man who holds my bags but doesn't burn. Oh, wait, there he is.

Now the geese are flying high again, berating the sky for inducing a panic state, clouds like pillows shredded. I know I lack charisma, which is not a character flaw, per se, but my fate doesn't suit me, nor does it suit the chainsaw incorporated into my song. When I die, the world will be a ghost town, replete with cowboy shoot ups. My past lives will all have swinging doors, and I won't regret leaving my darlings on the edge of the material world. Speak to the magician. He's a juice box, juice box, juice box johnny, and I am the sorry one.

The Olympic village, the athletes, the muscle mass weighing down the mountain make me sleep standing up. It's the only way to tap into that lightening mind, that key on the kite string, that God reservoir. My only reservation is the flourish on my signature. It's a dunking tank danger zone with one too many characters. I remember the paralysis, the lockjaw. And Lionel, the lion man. The problem isn't unhappy endings. It's too many happy endings with no place to begin.

I'm being followed by those dog-eared, bleary-eyed, epistolary days. They bring me pills in dixie cups while I danced a funny polka to ferry the ghosts back into the glory while a black hole tortures the room with its gravity. Lifting off again, nano arms, looking for a body that can handle them, but I can't seem to manage the size I am now, these god-sized brains, these god-sized brains.

Not a Walk on the Beach

The air before me
is the flavor of
an oat cake popsicle.
Or a shoe box.
Or the water sports
I'm not doing.
So I sign for
a prescription
while all the world
is water sporting
in brightly-colored
board shorts. It's
a matter of geometry—
every body on the beach
is a perfect angle. They
lean toward life. They
lean toward classified
water sports while
I decide to buy
a frozen thing and
enter ghost
exhalation.
In this place, ghosts
are not much
to talk about.
Boating,
now there's a good
topic for conversation.
On a motor boat, on
a reservoir as dull
as the beer cans

that bob in it,
mouths opens
but only motor
sounds come out.
Longing for death
is like stumbling
through the freezer aisle
in a wet bathing suit
clutching chicken
cutlets shaped like
guns. But the
crushed head of an
accidental fall never
manifests. The floor
is too aloof today.
Still my need to
climb into the freezer.
It's a matter of not
fitting in. Or a
personification
problem. Or perhaps
it's the prescription.
Boats pull away
from a dock
somewhere and press
their faces into
the water. It's
the water that makes
them sicker.
Or perhaps
it's the chicken.
There's a room

beneath the water
where all the guns
are hidden in
the game system.
All the grunts and
all the guns. And
no one water-skis in
the game system.
No one is having any fun.

To the Actor Who Plays Me in an Educational Video

It's important to be
nervous.   Channel uneven
washing machine.   Take advantage
of your props.   Slip an arm
into a sweater sleeve.
Remove your shoes.   Remove
your feet.
Don't linger over
magazine cover of volcano.   Don't forget
this is your planet.
Because your time here
is short-lived.   Unravel sweater threads.
Embroider doctor's coat with jungle cats.
If you wave at the lion   and the lion
doesn't come,   remember,
you will fail.   Remember,
your failure will benefit
this unnamed planet,   where, yes,
it's very hot.   Remove
your sweater.
The oceans boil all the time here.
There are vents   to release the steam
with cameras in them.   Forget
that you are being
watched.   Forget that you are visible.
Then spill your plans   with shaky hands.
I will now put on my sweater.
Remember
there will be no ransom.   Remember
a rooftop chase is inevitable.

Disembarkation

"I never heard the word bomb until the FBI asked me did you hear the word bomb?"
—a witness interviewed after the shooting of Rigoberto Alpizar by Federal Air Marshalls

1.

They say it was somewhere
between three and nine.

Three and nine birds?
No, bullets.

They flew across the aisle
like egrets? No, bullets.

It's so typical of bullets
to be so unaccountable.

They are packed in chambers
by robots with stovepipe arms.

Please don't be alarmed
at being human.

2.

If it's day, let the agents have a head start   you don't want
to be accused of being a sore loser   when the sonic airtight
container snaps over the dome of your head   you might regret
helping with your ailing mother as the shots are fired
you might have been good at something   in addition to
raising a periscope to listen.

3.

They say you're supposed to make yourself
as big as possible
when threatened.

See the egret in the field, see the wolf pack circling,
see the egret
spread its wings.

He's sick, he's sick, he's sick!

See the words on an backpack,   the words
on an eyelid,   the words
on a coffee mug:

"Welcome to Miami."

4.

If it's night, don't believe anything you see   the best art is hidden
in museums   it's sealed in and though you wish you were
among its skies and faces   the robots came along   all shiny
they carried boxes in their stovepipe arms   boxes filled with
bullets   or was it egrets?

5.

When you leave a ship or plane or blimp
do you believe   in shaking
before   the godless face of robots?
There's a sophisticated screen ahead.
All the words are falling   like rain.
Not dancing,   not cart-wheeling,   just
falling,   you can read them if you want,
all the cities   you can think of, just like
your tired eyes scan family photo albums.
You think of all those decades   you
lost yourself   between the sky and sky.
You don't want to fall,   don't have wings.
Jet way,   jet bridge, air bridge, de-plane,

unboard,   gateway,   tunnel. Even birds
forget their names sometimes.

6.

Do you dream those impossible dreams like I do?
The ones where you're walking alone
in the cemetery?

The seat backs looked like gravestones
so you designed an epitaph while
your mother stirred the sauce for dinner.

You had a glum face, she let you
have your glum face.
She's dead now; she's somewhere in this cemetery.

This happens
in a flash, but this is not your childhood, it's
a crowd-sourced childhood

for every child who has sacrificed themselves
to the robots.
Did you know that egrets have very few predators

due to their tremendous wing spans?
You spread your wings as you de-plane.
Though you can't put people back together,

you can now look birds in the face
and claim that you're from everywhere
the bullets aren't.

Dialectical Argument with Boyfriend and Birdkiller

See the braided bowl of bird intestines
on the bed pillow and the twig of leg on the stairwell?
Let's talk about my death as a pardonable offense.
Do you really wish you didn't have a head?   If   then
the cat won't go outside   bird murder
haunts his haunches.
I pretend to have a hurt wing as I'm channel surfing.
Oh, you're watching too much Animal Planet.   But
the hatchet in the trunk,   there's nothing worse
than a chopped up version of yourself.   What if I
plummet?   What if I   in the wide-eyed chasm
party without panties on   or worse?
Every day,   you say,   *every day I recommend,*
try a little of this blue hair.   *We can grow old.*
We can drive the car to Walmart.   *Even parking lots*
are somewhere.   But
sometimes I can't follow what's happening on *Friends*.
I worry too much about their rents increasing.
Do they die in the end?   No spoilers!

Behind the Century

[Google Street View of 525 S Sable, Aurora CO, June 2012]

Behind the Century's horizon,
empty parking lot,   blue sky,
                braced breath.

Up the road, there's
a gap where   the wires aren't
strung across   the door jamb yet
and guns
are   being loaded.

Enter

the vacant lot   across the street.
It can hurt
when you consider
it's lack   of stadium seating

and
the voices tossed
from passing cars:
what do you want to see today?

We cannot dismiss
the sun scatter high above   the radial
elements   spinning down into
a green culvert
what kind of tree is that?   Tiny beetles in
ground fur.   It was the same

one hundred years ago.   The paper sound of wasps
building their closest guess
at heaven   in a dry creek bed,   the subtle click
of regurgitating   clouds.

Meanwhile,

the nail ghosts hammer too loudly
across town.

Meanwhile,

why must there be
a meanwhile?

Delusions of Reference in a Dark Room

When a ghost in this room is a sign of a ghost
in another room.   When ceiling cracks
are a sign that the continent will crumble.
When the water in a glass   is the water
that will drown us.
When this building tells me everything about
another building.   When a person in the room
is not a person,   they are a building on fire.
When the windows   do not open.
When my eyelid   is not
a fire extinguisher,   it is
an anti-smoking pamphlet.   When I cannot
read instructions.   When all my clothes
have prophecies stitched into them like zippers.
When zippers
do not open.   When they gnash their teeth
at blankets.   Then I glance at the flowers
someone placed beside my bed.   A petal falls
and the universe reaches its natural conclusion.

Notes

The painting referenced in "Gericault Paints a Portrait of a Woman Suffering from Obsessive Envy" comes from the series *Portraits of the Insane* that was commissioned from Theodore Gericault in 1822 to illustrate how appearance could be used as a diagnostic method for insanity.

The epigraph from Agamemnon in "The Furies Leave Los Angeles" is from the translation by Anne Carson.

"Disembarkation" was written after the shooting of Rigoberto Alpizar who had a manic episode on a plane and was shot in the back by Federal Air Marshalls while his wife yelled out, "He's sick!"

The address in the epigraph of "Behind the Century" is the location of the movie theater where the Aurora shooting took place. The poem is a memorial to those who died in the shooting. The shooter, James Eagan Holmes, told his psychiatrist he was hearing voices and having homicidal thoughts before the shooting took place, but he wasn't committed. This is a terrible tragedy for all involved, and I deeply wish it could have been prevented.

Jennifer Metsker is the Writing Coordinator at the Stamps School of Art & Design. She received her MFA in Poetry from the University of Michigan and studied painting at the School of the Art Institute of Chicago. Her poetry has been published in *Beloit Poetry Review*, *The Southern Review*, *The Michigan Quarterly Review*, *Gulf Coast*, *Rhino*, *Cream City Review*, *Birdfeast* and many other journals. She has also had poetry published on *Verse Daily* and *Poetry Daily*. Her audio poetry has been featured on the BBC radio program *Short Cuts*.

The New Issues Editor's Choice